Great-Grandfather

Great-Grandfather

Great-Grandmother

Great-Grandmother

Grandfather

Grandmother

Father

Family Tree

Great-Grandfather

Great-Grandfather

Great-Grandmother

Great-Grandmother

Grandfather

Grandmother

Mother

Me

This book contains

the memories and traditions of the

_____Family

What a treasure-house filled with rare jewels
are the blessings of year after year
When life has been lived as we've lived it
in a home where God's presence is dear.

The Helen Steiner Rice Foundation

When someone does a kindness,
   it always seems to me
That's the way God up in heaven
   would like us all to be,
For when we bring some pleasure
   to another human heart,
We have followed in His footsteps
   and we've had a little part
In serving Him who loves us,
   and I'm very sure it's true,
That in serving those around us
   we serve and please Him too.

Whatever the celebration, whatever the day, whatever the event, whatever the occasion, Helen Steiner Rice possessed the ability to express the appropriate feeling for that particular moment in time.

A happening became happier, a sentiment more sentimental, a memory more memorable because of her deep sensitivity to put into understandable language the emotion being experienced. Her positive attitude, her concern for others, and her love of God are identifiable threads woven into her life, her work . . . and even her death.

Prior to Mrs. Rice's passing, she established the Helen Steiner Rice Foundation, a nonprofit corporation that awards grants to worthy charitable programs assisting the elderly and the needy. Royalties from the sale of this book will add to the financial capabilities of the Helen Steiner Rice Foundation. Because of limited resources, the foundation presently limits grants to qualified charitable programs in Lorain, Ohio, where Helen Steiner Rice was born, and Greater Cincinnati, Ohio, where Mrs. Rice lived and worked most of her life. Hopefully in the future, resources will be of sufficient size that broader geographical areas may be considered in the awarding of grants.

Because of her foresight, caring, and deep conviction of sharing, Helen Steiner Rice continues to touch a countless number of lives through grants and through her inspirational poetry.

Andrea R. Cornett, Administrator

Our Family Treasury

Helen Steiner Rice
and Virginia Juergens Ruehlmann

Fleming H. Revell
A Division of Baker Book House
Grand Rapids, Michigan 49516

© 1998 by Virginia J. Ruehlmann and
The Helen Steiner Rice Foundation

Published by Fleming H. Revell
a division of Baker Book House Company
P.O. Box 6287, Grand Rapids, MI 49516-6287

Second printing, July 1998

Printed in the United States of America

ISBN 0-8007-1732-5

Background pattern © CONCORD Fabrics, Pattern 875.

For current information about all releases from Baker Book House, visit our web site:
http://www.bakerbooks.com

To

The members
of our family

They have created a legacy of
happy happenings—
precious moments of the past,
timeless treasures of today,
and tender hopes and dreams
for tomorrow.
Truly
a heritage of
heartfelt and lasting love.

Introduction

A family is united firmly
   with a love that's deep and true,
The past is woven with memories
   and filled with traditions too.
Reminisce and travel back
   and those precious times review,
And may your family's memories
   bring forth a smile or two.

               VJR

    The family is the most important unit of our society. The stability and advancement of a community, a city, a state, a nation depend on the strength of the family unit. The ideals of faith, hope, and love originate and are nurtured, encouraged, and maintained in the family. Indeed, these virtures are woven into the fabric of a family.

    May this book help you and your family remember with fondness the days and experiences within your family circle. Treasure the good times, learn from those not so happy times, and pass on the heritage of warmth, love, memories, examples, and fond recollections.

                          Sincerely,
                    Virginia J. Ruehlmann

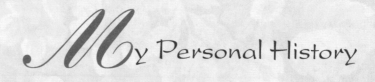

My Personal History

Biographical information

Name

Birth date

Place

City   State

Attending doctor

Weight   Height

Color of eyes   Color of hair

Most distinguishing feature or characteristic

Birth order

Spouse

Current address

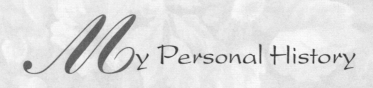

My Personal History

Education

Elementary _____

High school _____

College _____

Graduate school _____

Work experience

First job _____ Dates _____

   Employer _____

   Best thing about the job _____

   Most recent pace of employment _____

   Position held _____ Dates _____

   Best thing about the job _____

   Most memorable achievement on the job _____

Religious background

Churches attended _____

Church involvement _____

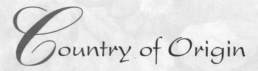

Country of Origin

Mother's Side

Country

City

Family heritage

Date ancestors immigrated

Who made the journey

Mode of transportation

Route

Reasons for immigrating

Time cannot be halted
    in its swift and endless flight,
For age is sure to follow youth
    like day comes after night.

Country of Origin

Father's Side

Country _____

City _____

Family heritage _____

Date ancestors immigrated _____

Who made the journey _____

_____

_____

Mode of transportation _____

_____

Route _____

_____

Reasons for immigrating _____

_____

_____

_____

Looking back across the years
it's a joy to reminisce,
For memory opens wide the door
on a happy day like this.

Biographical information

Name

Birth date

Place

City   State

Attending doctor

Weight   Height

Color of eyes   Color of hair

Most distinguishing feature or characteristic

Birth order

May memory open your heart's door wide
And make you a child at your mother's side.

Family members

Mother _____

Father _____

Sisters _____

Brothers _____

Grandparents _____

Special friends

_____

_____

Pets

_____

_____

Addresses of childhood homes

_____

_____

_____

_____

Bless Mother's dear heart with insight to see
Her love means more than the world to me.

Education

Elementary

High school

College

Graduate school

Work experience

First job   Dates

  Employer

  Best thing about the job

Most recent place of employment

  Position held   Dates

  Best thing about the job

  Most memorable achievement on the job

A mother's love is like a beacon,
  burning bright with faith and prayer,
And through the changing scenes of life,
  we find a haven there.

Churches attended _____

Church involvement _____

Membership in organizations _____

Volunteer work _____

Most significant accomplishment _____

Best advice _____

Pet peeve _____

Favorites

   Hobby _____   Color _____

   Sport _____   Author _____

   Song _____   Musician _____

   Movie _____

   Means of relaxation _____

   Expression _____

   Scripture verse _____

No one gives more happiness or does more good for others
Than understanding, kind, and selfless loving mothers.

Biographical information

Name

Birth date

Place

City   State

Attending doctor

Weight   Height

Color of eyes   Color of hair

Most distinguishing feature or characteristic

Birth order

Fathers are just wonderful
in a million different ways.
They merit loving compliments
and accolades of praise.

 *Father*

Family members

Mother

Father

Sisters

Brothers

Grandparents

Special friends

Pets

Addresses of childhood homes

Precious little memories of small things Dad has done,
Make the very darkest day a bright and happy one.

Father

Education

Elementary

High school

College

Graduate school

Work experience

First job   Dates

  Employer

  Best thing about the job

Most recent place of employment

  Position held   Dates

  Best thing about the job

  Most memorable achievement on the job

Dad, may you always realize
that your children and their children too
Care for you and love you
just because you're you.

Father

Churches attended

Church involvement

Membership in organizations

Volunteer work

Most significant accomplishment

Best advice

Pet peeve

Favorites

Hobby   Color

Sport   Author

Song   Musician

Movie

Means of relaxation

Expression

Scripture verse

Like our Heavenly Father, Dad's a guardian and guide,
Someone we can count on to be always on our side.

19

Mother and Father's Dating Years

First time they met _____

Place _____

How they met _____

_____

_____

First date _____

_____

_____

Place _____

_____

First kiss _____

Special song _____

Favorite movie _____

Favorite date _____

_____

_____

Favorite foods _____

Closest friends _____

_____

_____

Blessed little memories
of happiness and love
Are gifts to keep forever
from our Father up above.

Mother and Father's Wedding

Their wedding was held on _____ (date) at _____ (time)

at _____ (place)

The wedding party

Matron or maid of honor _____

Bridesmaids _____

Best man _____

Groomsmen _____

Other participants _____

Clergy _____

Musicians _____

Special readings _____

Songs _____

Color scheme and flowers _____

Location of reception _____

Menu _____

First song requested _____

Special guests attending _____

Honeymoon _____

_____

It seems like only yesterday you were a radiant bride,
With a proud and happy bridegroom standing at your side.

21

Mother and Father's World

The year they were married . . .

Prices

    Loaf of bread   Pound of hamburger

    Quart of milk   Rent for an apartment

    Newspaper   New home

    Gallon of gasoline   New car

    Ice-cream cone   Hourly wage

President of country

Events in the news

Sports heroes

Entertainers

Popular music groups

Clothing styles

      Look back across the years now fled,
      Remember together the day you wed.
      So much has happened, so much has changed
      Since the day your vows were pledged and exchanged.

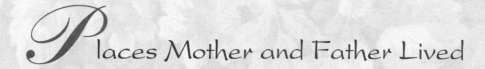# Places Mother and Father Lived

First home

Location

Characteristics of home

Home where they raised their children

Location

Characteristics of home

Other homes in which they lived

Location

Characteristics of home

Location

Characteristics of home

Home where they retired

Location

Characteristics of home

In seeking peace for all people, there is only one place to begin,
And that is in each heart and home, for the fortress of peace is within.

$\mathcal{M}$other and Father's Children

Name

Birth date   Day   Time

City   County   State

Weight   Height

Baptism or dedication date

Place

Clergy

Name

Birth date   Day   Time

City   County   State

Weight   Height

Baptism or dedication date

Place

Clergy

Name

Birth date   Day   Time

City   County   State

Weight   Height

Baptism or dedication date

Place

Clergy

A baby is a gift of life, born of the wonder of love—
A little bit of eternity sent from the Father above.

$\mathcal{M}$other and Father's Children

Name

Birth date   Day   Time

City   County   State

Weight   Height

Baptism or dedication date

Place

Clergy

Name

Birth date   Day   Time

City   County   State

Weight   Height

Baptism or dedication date

Place

Clergy

Name

Birth date   Day   Time

City   County   State

Weight   Height

Baptism or dedication date

Place

Clergy

Mother and Father's Children

Name _____

Birth date _____ Day _____ Time _____

City _____ County _____ State _____

Weight _____ Height _____

Baptism or dedication date _____

Place _____

Clergy _____

Name _____

Birth date _____ Day _____ Time _____

City _____ County _____ State _____

Weight _____ Height _____

Baptism or dedication date _____

Place _____

Clergy _____

Name _____

Birth date _____ Day _____ Time _____

City _____ County _____ State _____

Weight _____ Height _____

Baptism or dedication date _____

Place _____

Clergy _____

Mother and Father's Grandchildren

Name

Birth date   Place

Parents

Name

Birth date   Place

Parents

Name

Birth date   Place

Parents

Name

Birth date   Place

Parents

Name

Birth date   Place

Parents

Mother and Father's Grandchildren

Name _____

Birth date _____ Place _____

Parents _____

Name _____

Birth date _____ Place _____

Parents _____

Name _____

Birth date _____ Place _____

Parents _____

Name _____

Birth date _____ Place _____

Parents _____

Name _____

Birth date _____ Place _____

Parents _____

There's nothing like a grandchild to boast of and adore
And to bring back precious memories of babyhood once more.

Mother and Father's Grandchildren

Name _____

Birth date _____ Place _____

Parents _____

Name _____

Birth date _____ Place _____

Parents _____

Name _____

Birth date _____ Place _____

Parents _____

Name _____

Birth date _____ Place _____

Parents _____

Name _____

Birth date _____ Place _____

Parents _____

Name _____

Birth date _____ Place _____

Parents _____

Mother and Father's Grandchildren

Name _____

Birth date _____ Place _____

Parents _____

Name _____

Birth date _____ Place _____

Parents _____

Name _____

Birth date _____ Place _____

Parents _____

Name _____

Birth date _____ Place _____

Parents _____

Name _____

Birth date _____ Place _____

Parents _____

Memories of thoughtful acts grandchildren have done
Make each day together a bright and happy one.

Mother and Father's Grandchildren

Name _____

Birth date _____ Place _____

Parents _____

Name _____

Birth date _____ Place _____

Parents _____

Name _____

Birth date _____ Place _____

Parents _____

Name _____

Birth date _____ Place _____

Parents _____

Name _____

Birth date _____ Place _____

Parents _____

With loving wishes comes a deep and heartfelt prayer—
God, keep our grandchildren safely in Your care.

Grandmother and Grandfather

Mother's side of the family

Name

Birth date   Place

Interesting facts

Name

Birth date   Place

Interesting facts

Where they lived most of their lives

What they did most of their lives

Remember when Grandma . . .

Remember when Grandpa . . .

The door to your heart and home stood open with welcoming cheer,
And memories of you, Grandma, grow deeper with each year.

Grandmother and Grandfather

Father's side of the family

Name _____

Birth date _____ Place _____

Interesting facts _____

_____

Name _____

Birth date _____ Place _____

Interesting facts _____

_____

_____

Where they lived most of their lives _____

What they did most of their lives _____

_____

_____

Remember when Grandma . . . _____

_____

_____

Remember when Grandpa . . . _____

_____

_____

If you look inside of Grandpa's heart, where no one else can see,
You'll find he's sentimental and as soft as he can be.

33

Great-Grandmother and Great-Grandfather

Mother's side of the family

Name

Birth date   Place

Interesting facts

Name

Birth date   Place

Interesting facts

Name

Birth date   Place

Interesting facts

Name

Birth date   Place

Interesting facts

Wish they could tell us about . . .

Great-Grandmother and Great-Grandfather

Father's side of the family

Name

Birth date   Place

Interesting facts

Name

Birth date   Place

Interesting facts

Name

Birth date   Place

Interesting facts

Name

Birth date   Place

Interesting facts

Wish they could tell us about . . .

Birthday traditions

Birthdays are gateways between old years and new,
Just openings to the future where we get a wider view.

Special birthdays celebrated

Person _____ Birthday _____

Festivities _____

_____

Person _____ Birthday _____

Festivities _____

_____

Person _____ Birthday _____

Festivities _____

_____

Person _____ Birthday _____

Festivities _____

_____

Person _____ Birthday _____

Festivities _____

Birthdays are doorways to what the future holds
And to greater understanding as the story of life unfolds.

Weddings

Bride _____   Groom _____
Date _____   Location _____

Bride _____   Groom _____
Date _____   Location _____

Bride _____   Groom _____
Date _____   Location _____

Bride _____   Groom _____
Date _____   Location _____

Bride _____   Groom _____
Date _____   Location _____

Bride _____   Groom _____
Date _____   Location _____

Bride _____   Groom _____
Date _____   Location _____

May God bless your wedding day
and every day thereafter
And fill your home with happiness,
your hearts with love and laughter.

Weddings

Bride _____   Groom _____
Date _____   Location _____

Bride _____   Groom _____
Date _____   Location _____

Bride _____   Groom _____
Date _____   Location _____

Bride _____   Groom _____
Date _____   Location _____

Bride _____   Groom _____
Date _____   Location _____

Bride _____   Groom _____
Date _____   Location _____

Bride _____   Groom _____
Date _____   Location _____

Oh, God of love, look down and bless
this radiant pair with happiness
And grant that they may always stay
as joyful as they are today.

*S*pecial Anniversaries

Name _____

Date _____ Occasion _____

Name _____

Date _____ Occasion _____

Name _____

Date _____ Occasion _____

Name _____

Date _____ Occasion _____

Name _____

Date _____ Occasion _____

Name _____

Date _____ Occasion _____

Name _____

Date _____ Occasion _____

Name _____

Date _____ Occasion _____

A husband and wife sharing smiles and tears
Build up rich treasures all their married years.

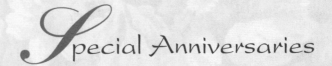

Special Anniversaries

Name

Date   Occasion

Name

Date   Occasion

Name

Date   Occasion

Name

Date   Occasion

Name

Date   Occasion

Name

Date   Occasion

Name

Date   Occasion

Name

Date   Occasion

May all the love and tenderness of married years well spent
Come back today to fill your heart and make you feel content.

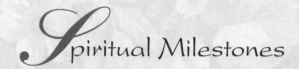

Spiritual Milestones

Baptism, dedication, confirmation,
communion, spiritual decisions

Name _____ Event _____
Place _____ Date _____

Name _____ Event _____
Place _____ Date _____

Name _____ Event _____
Place _____ Date _____

Name _____ Event _____
Place _____ Date _____

Name _____ Event _____
Place _____ Date _____

Name _____ Event _____
Place _____ Date _____

Name _____ Event _____
Place _____ Date _____

There is nothing that can compare
With knowing we are in God's care.

42

 Spiritual Milestones

Baptism, dedication, confirmation,
communion, spiritual decisions

Name _____ Event _____
Place _____ Date _____

Name _____ Event _____
Place _____ Date _____

Name _____ Event _____
Place _____ Date _____

Name _____ Event _____
Place _____ Date _____

Name _____ Event _____
Place _____ Date _____

Name _____ Event _____
Place _____ Date _____

Name _____ Event _____
Place _____ Date _____

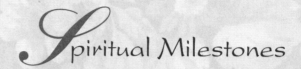

Spiritual Milestones

Baptism, dedication, confirmation,
communion, spiritual decisions

Name _____ Event _____
Place _____ Date _____

Name _____ Event _____
Place _____ Date _____

Name _____ Event _____
Place _____ Date _____

Name _____ Event _____
Place _____ Date _____

Name _____ Event _____
Place _____ Date _____

Name _____ Event _____
Place _____ Date _____

Name _____ Event _____
Place _____ Date _____

In His care we need not fear—
His presence fills our hearts with cheer.

*C*hristmas Celebrations

Traditional gathering place _____

Usual date _____ Time _____

Those usually present _____

_____

_____

Favorite variety of Christmas tree _____

Trimmings _____

_____

_____

Special ornaments _____

_____

Favorite decorations _____

_____

Menu _____

_____

_____

_____

Family traditions for celebration _____

_____

_____

_____

Memories to treasure are made on Christmas Day—
Made of family gatherings and children as they play.

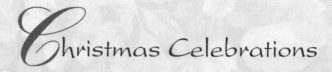

Christmas Celebrations

Favorite traditions

Church services attended on Christmas Eve or Christmas Day

Memorable Christmas programs

Activities following service

Most meaningful Christmas Day activities

Accept God's priceless gift of love, reach out and you'll receive.
The only payment that God asks is that you just believe.

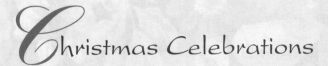
Christmas Celebrations

Favorite traditions

Christmas story read from

Read by

Favorite carols and songs

Song leader

Accompanists and instruments

Ritual for gift exchange

Memorable gifts given and received

As once more we celebrate the birth of our King,
Let us search our hearts for the best gift to bring.

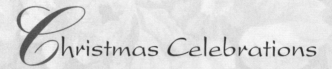

Christmas Celebrations

Favorite traditions

Special TV shows or movies enjoyed

Memorable Christmas Day activities (games, sledding, caroling)

Favorite Christmas musical recordings

Christmas is a lovely link
between old years and new
That keeps the bond of family love
forever strong and true.

Christmas Celebrations

Favorite Christmastime recipes

A star in the sky, an angel's voice
Telling the world, "Rejoice! Rejoice!"

Favorite Christmastime recipes

In our Christmas celebrations of merriment and mirth,
Let us not forget the miracle of the holy Christ Child's birth.

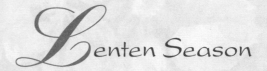

Lenten Season

Ash Wednesday

Observances

_____

_____

_____

Maundy Thursday

Observances

_____

_____

_____

Good Friday

Observances

_____

_____

_____

Before the dawn of Easter there came Gethsemane.
Before the resurrection, there were hours of agony.

Celebration begins with _____

Traditional gathering place _____

Menu _____

_____

_____

Most memorable Easter _____

_____

_____

Traditions _____

_____

_____

_____

_____

Easter is a season of joy and hope and cheer.
There's beauty all around us to see and touch and hear.

Favorite recipes

Long, long ago in a land far away,
There came the dawn of the first Easter Day.

Mother's Day

Celebration begins with _____

Traditional gathering place _____

Menu _____

_____

_____

Most memorable Mother's Day _____

_____

_____

_____

_____

Traditions _____

_____

_____

_____

_____

Mother's Day is remembrance day,
and we pause on the path of the year
To honor and bring loving tribute to
the mother our hearts hold dear.

Father's Day

Celebration begins with _____

Traditional gathering place _____

Menu _____

_____

_____

Most memorable Father's Day _____

_____

_____

_____

_____

Traditions _____

_____

_____

_____

_____

Father's Day is one of those days
When Dad deserves some extra praise.
Dad, you're kind and thoughtful too.
More dads should be modeled after you.

55

Thanksgiving

Celebration begins with

Traditional gathering place
Menu

Most memorable Thanksgiving

Traditions

Favorite recipe

Thank you, God, for little things that often come our way—
The things we take for granted and don't mention when we pray.

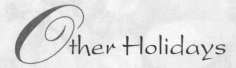

Other Holidays

New Year's Eve and New Year's Day

Traditional activities

Valentine's Day

Traditional activities

Presidents' Day

Traditional activities

Memorial Day

Traditional activities

Flag Day

Traditional activities

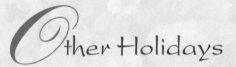

Fourth of July

Traditional activities

Labor Day

Traditional activities

Halloween

Traditional activities

Memorable costumes

Special parties

Veterans' Day

Traditional activities

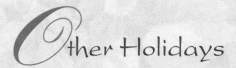

ther Holidays

Martin Luther King Day, Kwanza, Passover,
Yom Kippur, Rosh Hashanah, Hanukkah

Traditional activities

Special foods

Great is our gladness to serve God through others,
For our Father taught us we are all sisters and brothers.

*M*emorable Springtimes

Location _____

Year _____

Description _____

_____

_____

_____

Location _____

Year _____

Description _____

_____

_____

_____

Location _____

Year _____

Description _____

_____

_____

All nature heeds the call of spring
As God awakens everything.

$\mathscr{M}$emorable Summertimes

Location
Year
Description

Location
Year
Description

Location
Year
Description

Spring always comes with new life and birth,
Followed by summer to warm the soft earth.
And, oh, what a comfort to know there are reasons
That souls, like nature, must too have their seasons.

*M*emorable Autumns

Location _____
Year _____
Description _____

_____

Location _____
Year _____
Description _____

_____

Location _____
Year _____
Description _____

_____

What a wonderful time is life's autumn
when the leaves of the trees are all gold,
When God fills each day, as He sends it,
with memories, priceless and old.

$\mathcal{M}$emorable Winters

Location _____

Year _____

Description _____

_____

_____

Location _____

Year _____

Description _____

_____

_____

Location _____

Year _____

Description _____

_____

_____

In the beauty of a snowflake
falling softly on the land,
Is the mystery and the miracle
of God's great, creative hand.

 Graduations

Name   Date
Institution
Activities

Name   Date
Institution
Activities

Name   Date
Institution
Activities

Name   Date
Institution
Activities

Name   Date
Institution
Activities

As you go on from graduation, take faith along with you,
And great will be your happiness as your dearest dream comes true.

*G*raduations

Name   Date

Institution

Activities

Name   Date

Institution

Activities

Name   Date

Institution

Activities

Name   Date

Institution

Activities

Name   Date

Institution

Activities

Name   Date

Institution

Activities

Honors and Accomplishments

Name   Date
Honor or award

Name   Date
Honor or award

Name   Date
Honor or award

Name   Date
Honor or award

Name   Date
Honor or award

Name   Date
Honor or award

Name   Date
Honor or award

Name   Date
Honor or award

Honors and Accomplishments

Name _____ Date _____
Honor or award _____

Name _____ Date _____
Honor or award _____

Name _____ Date _____
Honor or award _____

Name _____ Date _____
Honor or award _____

Name _____ Date _____
Honor or award _____

Name _____ Date _____
Honor or award _____

Name _____ Date _____
Honor or award _____

Name _____ Date _____
Honor or award _____

Vacations

Year   Place
Transportation
Family members participating

Activities

Year   Place
Transportation
Family members participating

Activities

Year   Place
Transportation
Family members participating

Activities

Year   Place

Transportation

Family members participating

Activities

Year   Place

Transportation

Family members participating

Activities

Most memorable vacation

Most enjoyable vacation

We all need short vacations in life's fast and maddening race,
An interlude of relaxation from the constant, jet-age pace.

Serving Our Country

Name _____ Branch of Service _____

Dates _____ World situation _____

Name _____ Branch of Service _____

Dates _____ World situation _____

Name _____ Branch of Service _____

Dates _____ World situation _____

Name _____ Branch of Service _____

Dates _____ World situation _____

Name _____ Branch of Service _____

Dates _____ World situation _____

Name _____ Branch of Service _____

Dates _____ World situation _____

Name _____ Branch of Service _____

Dates _____ World situation _____

Everything worth having demands work and sacrifice,
And freedom is a gift from God that commands the highest price.

Illnesses

Name _____ Date _____
Illness _____

Name _____ Date _____
Illness _____

Name _____ Date _____
Illness _____

Name _____ Date _____
Illness _____

Name _____ Date _____
Illness _____

Name _____ Date _____
Illness _____

Name _____ Date _____
Illness _____

In sickness or health, in suffering and pain,
In storm-laden skies, in sunshine and rain,
God is always there to lighten your way
And lead you through darkness to a much brighter day.

Treasures and Heirlooms

Item _____ Purchase date _____

Original owner _____

Current owner _____

Treasured because _____

_____

_____

Item _____ Purchase date _____

Original owner _____

Current owner _____

Treasured because _____

_____

_____

Item _____ Purchase date _____

Original owner _____

Current owner _____

Treasured because _____

_____

_____

Teach me to give of myself in whatever way I can
Of whatever I have to give.

72

Treasures and Heirlooms

Item _____   Purchase date _____

Original owner _____

Current owner _____

Treasured because _____

_____

_____

Item _____   Purchase date _____

Original owner _____

Current owner _____

Treasured because _____

_____

_____

Item _____   Purchase date _____

Original owner _____

Current owner _____

Treasured because _____

_____

_____

Favorite Family Recipes

Recipe for _____

From _____

_____

_____

_____

_____

Recipe for _____

From _____

_____

_____

_____

_____

Take a cup of kindness, mix it well with love,
Add a lot of patience and faith in God above.

 avorite Family Recipes

Recipe for _____
From _____

_____
_____
_____
_____
_____
_____

Recipe for _____
From _____

_____
_____
_____
_____
_____
_____

Sprinkle very generously with joy and thanks and cheer,
And you'll have lots of "angel food" to feast on all the year.

Family Quotes and Anecdotes

Name
Quote

Name
Quote

Name
Quote

Name
Quote

Name
Quote

Name
Quote

Tender little memories of some kind word or deed
Give us strength and courage when we are in need.

Difficult situation _____

Family solved it by _____

_____

Lesson learned _____

_____

Difficult situation _____

Family solved it by _____

_____

Lesson learned _____

_____

Difficult situation _____

Family solved it by _____

_____

Lesson learned _____

_____

We all have cares and problems we cannot solve alone,
But if we go to God in prayer, we are never on our own.

Favorite Family Memories

Memories are treasures time cannot destroy—
They are happy pathways to yesterday's joy.

Family Reunions

Year _____ Location _____ Attendance _____

Memories _____

_____

_____

_____

Year _____ Location _____ Attendance _____

Memories _____

_____

_____

_____

Year _____ Location _____ Attendance _____

Memories _____

_____

_____

_____

Year _____ Location _____ Attendance _____

Memories _____

_____

_____

_____

Reunions come and reunions go and with them comes the thought
Of all the happy memories the passing years have brought.

Name _____
Relationship
Address _____
_____

Memorable occasions _____
_____
_____

Name _____
Relationship
Address _____
_____

Memorable occasions _____
_____
_____

Name _____
Relationship
Address _____
_____

Memorable occasions _____
_____
_____

Memories are treasures time cannot take away,
So may you be surrounded by happy ones today.

Relatives

Name _____
Relationship _____
Address _____
_____

Memorable occasions _____
_____
_____

Name _____
Relationship _____
Address _____
_____

Memorable occasions _____
_____
_____

Name _____
Relationship _____
Address _____
_____

Memorable occasions _____
_____
_____

With sweet nostalgia we longingly recall
The happy days of long ago that seem the best of all.

Relatives

Name
Relationship
Address

Memorable occasions

Name
Relationship
Address

Memorable occasions

Name
Relationship
Address

Memorable occasions

Make me feel much closer to those I'm fondest of,
And may they know I think of them with thankfulness and love.

Name _____

Relationship _____

Address _____

_____

Memorable occasions _____

_____

_____

Name _____

Relationship _____

Address _____

_____

Memorable occasions _____

_____

_____

Name _____

Relationship _____

Address _____

_____

Memorable occasions _____

_____

_____

Memories grow more meaningful with every passing year,
More precious and more beautiful, more treasured and more dear.

 *S*pecial Friends

Name _____
Special because _____
_____
_____
_____

Name _____
Special because _____
_____
_____
_____

Name _____
Special because _____
_____
_____
_____

Name _____
Special because _____
_____
_____
_____

Friendship is a priceless gift that can't be bought or sold.
To have an understanding friend is worth far more than gold.

Name
Special because

Name
Special because

Name
Special because

Name
Special because

Neighbors

Name _____

Neighborhood _____ Dates _____

Remembered because _____

_____

_____

_____

Name _____

Neighborhood _____ Dates _____

Remembered because _____

_____

_____

_____

Name _____

Neighborhood _____ Dates _____

Remembered because _____

_____

_____

_____

There are some folks we meet in passing
and forget them as soon as they go.
There are some we remember with pleasure
and feel honored and privileged to know.

86

$\mathcal{N}$eighbors

Name

Neighborhood   Dates

Remembered because

Name

Neighborhood   Dates

Remembered because

Name

Neighborhood   Dates

Remembered because

Church Friends

Name _____

Church _____ Dates _____

Remembered because _____

_____

_____

Name _____

Church _____ Dates _____

Remembered because _____

_____

_____

Name _____

Church _____ Dates _____

Remembered because _____

_____

_____

Happy little memories go flitting through my mind,
And in all my thoughts and memories I always seem to find
The picture of your face, the memory of your touch,
And all the other little things I've come to admire so much.

Church Friends

Name

Church   Dates

Remembered because

Name

Church   Dates

Remembered because

Name

Church   Dates

Remembered because

$\mathcal{R}$etirement Celebrations

Name _____ Date of retirement _____

Position held before retirement _____

Company _____

Activities during retirement _____

_____

_____

Name _____ Date of retirement _____

Position held before retirement _____

Company _____

Activities during retirement _____

_____

_____

Name _____ Date of retirement _____

Position held before retirement _____

Company _____

Activities during retirement _____

_____

_____

May the happy satisfaction of a splendid job well done
Help to make your earned retirement a very pleasant one.

90

$\mathcal{S}$pecial Events

Person	Date
Place	Event
Person	Date
Place	Event
Person	Date
Place	Event
Person	Date
Place	Event
Person	Date
Place	Event
Person	Date
Place	Event
Person	Date
Place	Event
Person	Date
Place	Event

*L*oved Ones Laid to Rest

Name _____ Date _____

Cemetery name and location

_____

Favorite memory

_____

_____

_____

Name _____ Date _____

Cemetery name and location

_____

Favorite memory

_____

_____

_____

Name _____ Date _____

Cemetery name and location

_____

Favorite memory

_____

_____

_____

After the night, the morning, bidding all darkness to cease.
After life's cares and sorrows, the comfort and sweetness of peace.

*L*oved Ones Laid to Rest

Name _____ Date _____

Cemetery name and location _____

_____

Favorite memory _____

_____

_____

_____

Name _____ Date _____

Cemetery name and location _____

_____

Favorite memory _____

_____

_____

_____

Name _____ Date _____

Cemetery name and location _____

_____

Favorite memory _____

_____

_____

_____

Like pilgrims we wander 'til death takes our hand
And we start our journey to God's Promised Land.

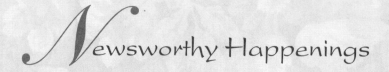 Newsworthy Happenings

Event _____

_____ Date _____

Importance _____

_____

Where I was when it happened _____

Event _____

_____ Date _____

Importance _____

_____

Where I was when it happened _____

Event _____

_____ Date _____

Importance _____

_____

Where I was when it happened _____

Event _____

_____ Date _____

Importance _____

_____

Where I was when it happened _____

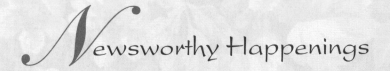

Newsworthy Happenings

Event _____

                                    Date _____

Importance _____

_____

Where I was when it happened _____

_____

Event _____

                                    Date _____

Importance _____

_____

Where I was when it happened _____

_____

Event _____

                                    Date _____

Importance _____

_____

Where I was when it happened _____

_____

Event _____

                                    Date _____

Importance _____

_____

Where I was when it happened _____

Things Unique to Our Family

Every family is different. No family heritage book can cover all the things that characterize your family and its history, so here is a blank page for you to use in describing that special uniqueness.